First published in Great Britain by
Macdonald and Co (Publishers) Ltd,
Greater London House, Hampstead Road, London NW1 7QX.

A TEMPLAR BOOK
Devised and produced by Templar Publishing Ltd,
Old King's Head Court, Dorking, Surrey.

ISBN 0-356-11639-5

Stidworthy, John
    The Human Ape?—(Creatures of the past;4)
    1. Human evolution—Juvenile literature
    I. Title   II. Series
    573.2   GN281

Series editor: A J Wood
Editor: Nicholas Bellenberg
Designer: Mike Jolley
Production: Sandra Bennigsen

Origination: Anglia Reproductions, Witham, Essex
Printing: Purnell Book Production Ltd, Paulton, Bristol
            Member of BPCC plc

PICTURE CREDITS
Pages 7: Michael Lyster/London Zoo
Page 12: John Reader
Pages 18-19: Bernard Wood/RIDA Photo Library
                The Photo Source
Page 25: COMPIX
Pages 26-27: John Frost Historical Newspaper Service
                The Mansell Collection
Pages 32-33: ZEFA
Page 36: The Research House/NASA

THE HUMAN APE?

Written by
JOHN STIDWORTHY
MA Cantab

Consultant Editor
STEVE PARKER
BSc Zoology

Illustrated by
CHRIS FORSEY

Macdonald

 **4,500 million**

 **600 million**

 **225 million**

 **65 million**

FIRST LIFE	PALEOZOIC	MESOZOIC

YEARS AGO

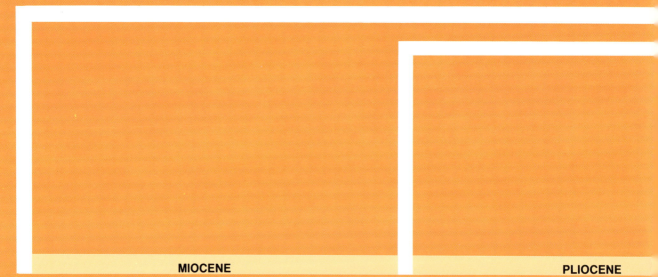

MIOCENE

PLIOCENE

26 million

7 million

Today

CENOZOIC

RECENT

PLEISTOCENE

2 million

100,000

Present

CONTENTS

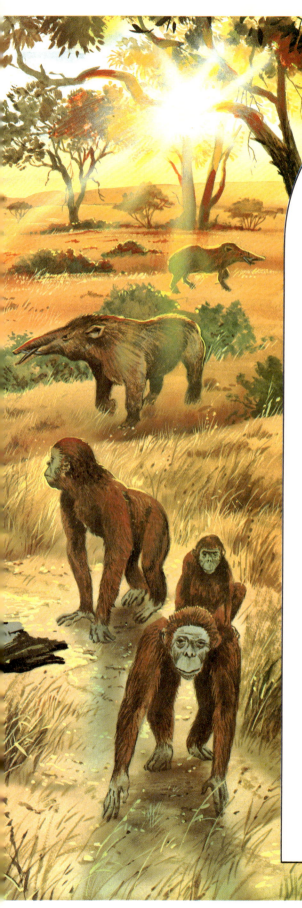

OUR DISTANT PAST

Humans belong to the ape group (called *Hominoidea*). We can begin the search for our evolutionary ancestors by looking for fossils of the first apes.

Fossils of various ape-like creatures have been found from the Miocene period, which began 26 million years ago. One of these was *Ramapithecus*, first found in India. Similar animals have also been found in other parts of Asia. They lived from about 14 million to about eight million years ago.

These early apes, often called 'ramapithecines', had certain similarities to humans. Whether they were our distant ancestors, we will probably never know. But they do give us an idea of how our ancestors might have evolved on the way to becoming human.

Ramapithecus lived at a time when the Earth's climate was becoming drier. The rain-loving forests that covered many tropical parts of the world were getting smaller, while grass-land 'savannahs', dotted with trees, were spreading. So the ramapithecines had to change with the times in order to survive.

Ramapithecines, like other apes, were designed mainly for climbing in trees. But as trees became less common they would have had to spend more time on the ground. Many scientists think that the change from tree-living to ground-dwelling set the ramapithecines (or creatures like them) on the evolutionary path which led to the first humans.

A little can say a lot

Most of the fossils of *Ramapithecus* that have been found so far are only tiny fragments. Just one or two teeth, possibly with the piece of jaw bone in which they were fixed. One of the most 'complete' finds is most of a lower jaw. Hardly any other parts of the skeleton have been discovered.

But how can we tell what the ramapithecines looked like, and how they lived, from these few bits and pieces? By comparing these fossils with the same parts of other, better-known creatures, a little can say a lot.

The number and shape of the teeth show that *Ramapithecus* was definitely a primate. That means it belonged to the group that includes monkeys, apes and humans. But were they more closely related to apes or to us? The shape of the jaw suggests that the ramapithecines were on our side of the family tree, as you can see on the far right.

The way the teeth wear down also tells more than you might think. Imagine yourself chewing a tough bit of food. Your jaw moves up and down – and also from side to side. So your teeth wear down in an even, flat way. Modern apes don't move their jaws from side to side, only up and down – partly because their long canine teeth would get in the way.

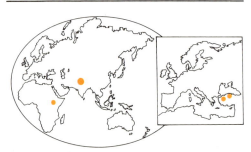

= Places where *Ramapithecus* remains have been found.

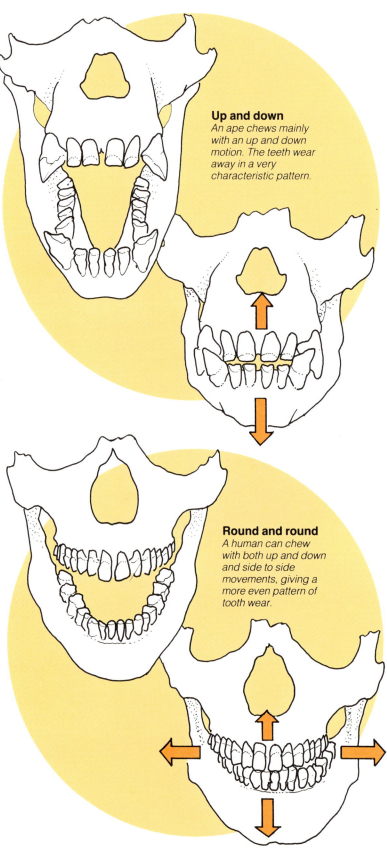

Up and down
An ape chews mainly with an up and down motion. The teeth wear away in a very characteristic pattern.

Round and round
A human can chew with both up and down and side to side movements, giving a more even pattern of tooth wear.

Their teeth wear down very unevenly, in grooves and pits. *Ramapithecus* teeth show a wear pattern that is more similar to our own than to a modern ape's.

Of course these clues only tell us that *Ramapithecus* was an ape-like creature from about 10 million years ago with jaws that looked and worked like ours.

But it's a far cry from knowing that this prehistoric creature was our ancestor. The problem is that the fossil evidence is so small and broken-up that scientists can interpret it in several ways. When a new tooth or bit of jaw turns up, more often than not it doesn't clarify matters, but just gives room for new arguments.

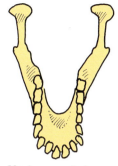

Modern ape's jaw
A modern ape such as a chimp has a large jaw that sticks out from the face. The sides of the jaw are parallel. The teeth, especially the canine teeth ('fangs'), are big in proportion to the jaw bone.

Human jaw
The jaw of a human is small and does not stick out much from the face. The sides of the jaw are not parallel – they form a curved shape. The teeth are quite small, and the canines aren't much bigger than the other teeth.

Before the chimp....

Proconsul is the name of a fossil ape from the Miocene period, about 20 million years ago. Its remains come from East Africa. This creature had many similarities to today's chimps. It was named after a very famous chimp called Consul who lived at London Zoo ('pro-' means 'before'). Like so many other fossil apes, its exact place in evolutionary history is uncertain. We are by no means sure that it was the ancestor of present-day chimps.

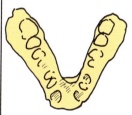

***Ramapithecus* jaw**
The ramapithecine jaw shows more similarities to a human than to a modern ape. It is not very large and its shape is more a curve, than the straight-sided U of an ape's jaw. The teeth are quite small too – the canines are only a little larger than the other teeth.

All apes together

We can look into the past, simply by looking around us today and finding animals that are similar to each other. Then we can try to work out which of their features have evolved recently, and which ones have been around for a long time – presumably inherited from a common ancestor.

There are five types of apes living today. One type is reading this – the human. The other four might qualify as being close relatives of ours. However the smallest apes, the gibbons of South-East Asia, are more monkey-like and are not generally thought to be very closely related to us. That leaves three others: orang-utans, chimps and gorillas.

Look at the pictures of these apes. You can immediately see obvious differences. Humans seem to have hardly any hair, while the others are quite furry. In fact this is not quite true. We actually have more hairs on our bodies than any of the other apes – but our hairs are much smaller and finer! So the nickname of the 'naked ape' for humans is not really correct.

There are plenty of other, more important, differences. We are upright, walking apes. The others are basically adapted for tree-climbing. Their arms are longer than their legs and they can swing through the trees with ease. They can grip with both their hands and their feet. When they move about on the ground it is usually on all fours, using their feet and the knuckles of

Today's apes
At first glance man looks very different from the other apes. But scientific study of bones, tissues and body chemistry shows that humans are very similar to chimps and gorillas.

Orang-utan

Gorilla

Gibbon

their hands. The shape of the hip bone reflects this way of getting about, as does the position of the head on the backbone. Most of these differences can be traced back to the time when pre-humans came down out of the trees.

It is important to remember that, just as the human species has evolved over the past few million years, so have the other apes. The popular idea of humans evolving from chimpanzees, or other apes or monkeys that are alive today, isn't true. They have changed from the common ancestor, just as we have.

Which of the apes alive today is our closest relative? The evidence can be interpreted in different ways. Overall, if you include similarities in body chemistry (see right), the chimp may be our closest living relative.

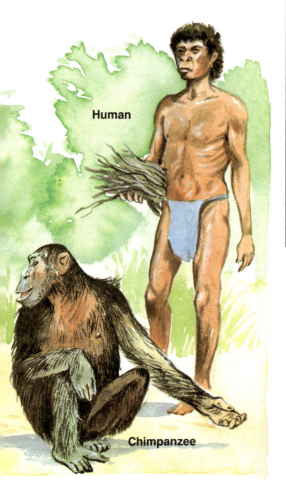

Human

Chimpanzee

Chemical clues

Many clues to evolution come from the shape and form of bones and other body parts. Recently scientists have come to realize that the 'shape' of chemical molecules inside the body can be just as revealing. The theory says the more similar a particular body chemical is in two animals, the more closely the animals are related.

For example, the chemical in blood called *haemoglobin*, carries oxygen from the lungs to all parts of the body. Haemoglobin has a complicated structure with over 500 'subunits', strung in lines like beads on lengths of string. The main form of haemoglobin in humans is identical to haemoglobin in chimpanzees. It is very unlikely that these haemoglobins evolved separately; it's much more probable that both humans and chimps inherited them from a common ancestor.

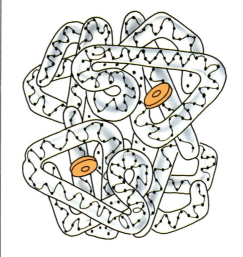

Haemoglobin molecule

The bigger brain

There are obvious differences in average brain size among the apes of today:

Gibbon ....about 90 mls (millilitres)
Chimp ....about 400 mls
Orang-utan ...about 450 mls
Gorilla ....about 500 mls
Human ....about 1300 mls

Even allowing for differences in body size, humans have by far the biggest brains in proportion to their bodies. Larger brains seem to be linked with greater intelligence. You can read about this on page 21.

Gibbon

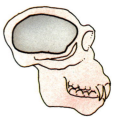

Chimpanzee

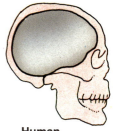

Human

A STEP CLOSER

By about four million years ago a new type of animal had evolved which had many human characteristics, although we would not call it human. This was *Australopithecus*, the 'southern ape'. Fossils of this creature have been found only in Africa.

Australopithecus had a fairly short muzzle (nose and mouth) compared to other apes, and its teeth had some human features. But it was only about the size of a chimpanzee, with a small brain – less than half the size of a human brain.

Some of the fossils are of the hip and leg bones. Their shapes show that *Australopithecus* could have walked comfortably on its legs alone. Apes walk awkwardly on their legs, and only for short distances. They prefer to shamble on all fours instead.

Any doubts about whether *Australopithecus* really could walk were swept away when a trail of fossil footprints was found at Laetoli, in Tanzania. These prints were left in mud about 3.7 million years ago by two *Australopithecus* individuals, as you can read on page 13.

Australopithecines were clearly neither humans nor apes, in the usual sense of the words. Some people call them 'ape-men' but this is not very scientific. So these creatures, and others similar enough to humans to be thought of as closely related to us, are included in the human family *Hominidae*. They are known as 'hominids'.

Ancestors of us all?

In 1924, in South Africa, Dr Raymond Dart found the first skull of *Australopithecus*. He soon realized its importance as one of the 'missing links' in the evolution of human beings. However, many of his fellow scientists were not convinced. They thought that the little skull, found in a quarry near Taungs, was of a type of chimpanzee. Other scientists unkindly called it 'Dart's baby'.

Today there is hardly any doubt that 'Dart's baby' was indeed a 'missing link'. Many fossils of *Australopithecus* and other prehumans and early humans have been dug up in East and South Africa.

One of the most famous and most complete specimens is also one of the oldest. This is 'Lucy', who lived about 3 million years ago in what is now Ethiopia. Her remains were discovered in 1974 by Dr Donald Johanson. What made them so exciting was that, besides the usual bits of teeth and skulls, there were also hip and limb bones. These showed Johanson that Lucy walked upright, or very nearly so.

Lucy shows a mixture of ape and human features. In particular, though, the hip bone is much more human than ape-like. So is the top of the femur (thigh bone). And the skull was sup-

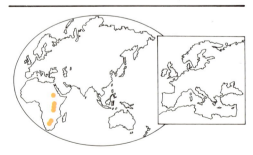

= Places where australopithecine fossils have been found.

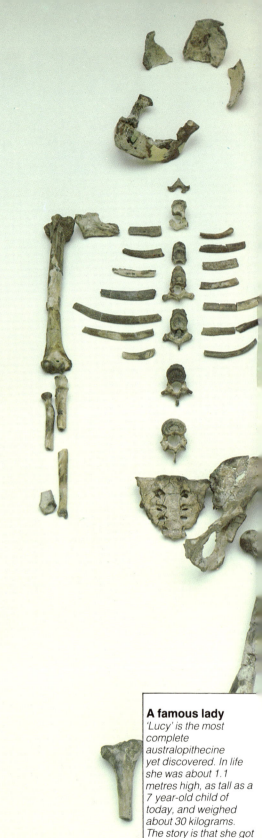

A famous lady
'Lucy' is the most complete australopithecine yet discovered. In life she was about 1.1 metres high, as tall as a 7 year-old child of today, and weighed about 30 kilograms. The story is that she got her nickname from the Beatles' song 'Lucy in the Sky with Diamonds', which was playing in the fossil-hunters' camp when her remains were found.

ported by the backbone from below, rather than at the back. There is little doubt Lucy could support all her weight on her legs and walk upright fairly easily.

Upright walking was, literally, a great stride forwards in evolution. The hands, freed from the need to help with movement by holding on to branches, could begin to explore, use and change objects. This ability may well have led to the evolution of a large brain and more intelligent behaviour, as you can read on page 21.

Some parts of Lucy were still rather ape-like. The head had a low forehead, large ridges over the eyebrows and a sticking-out jaw. Other parts were more human – the teeth were small and the jaw had a curved shape, not the straight-sided U of an ape.

As more australopithecine fossils are uncovered we can see that these hominids varied considerably. Different individuals seem to have a slightly different mix of features. We are almost certainly looking at more than one species. How many? You can find out on the next page.

Out for a stroll
The famous fossil footprints at Laetoli, mentioned on page 11, certainly show 'bipedal' locomotion' – walking on two legs. It cannot be proved that a creature like Lucy made them, but this seems extremely likely. Some scientists say the prints show signs of the toes curling. If so, this is an ape-like feature. Perhaps upright walking for an australopithecine was not quite as easy as it is for a modern human.

Human

Lucy

Gorilla

Femur Pelvis

Femur Pelvis

Pelvis

Femur

It's all in the hip!
Compare the tops of the thigh bones (called femurs) of a human, a gorilla and an australopithecine such as Lucy. In a human, the line of support goes straight up through the hip bone (pelvis) into the backbone. In a gorilla the femur is bent at an angle, since the ape tends to walk on all fours. Australopithecus had a femur much more like a human, which suggests upright walking.

Australopithecus afarensis

This is the earliest australopithecine species, to which Lucy belongs. Their fossils from East Africa date from 3.6 to 2.8 million years old. They were small – 1.1 to 1.2 metres tall, though larger specimens have been found that may have been the males of the species.

Australopithecus africanus

These remains are from 3 to 2.5 million years old and come from southern Africa. They were slightly larger than afarensis, *had bigger brains and their front teeth were slightly smaller.*

Australopithecus robustus

Fossils of this species come from South Africa and are about 2 to 1.5 million years old. They were heavily built creatures with large, powerful jaws and big cheek teeth, presumably for chewing tough plant food.

Australopithecus boisei

Remains of this hominid have been found in East Africa, where it lived around 1.8 million years ago. Its teeth and jaws were massive and even more adapted to chewing and grinding than robustus. *It has been nicknamed 'Nutcracker Man'.*

How many australopithecines?

The basic groups of living things are called species. The first thing to do with almost any plant or animal is find out which species it belongs to. With fossils, though, it is not always easy to tell how many different species you are dealing with.

The modern definition of a species is a group of animals (or plants) that can breed together, to produce offspring that can also breed. Of course, fossils don't breed!

All animals in a species usually look very similar. Tigers are big and have stripes. Leopards – a different species – are smaller and have spots. But fossils have neither spots nor stripes. We don't get many clues from fossil bones and teeth about general appearance. Faced with only a few bones which could be of a tiger or a leopard, telling which animal it is becomes much more difficult. Is it a large, heavily-built leopard or a small tiger?

In many fossil collections, then, it is difficult to decide how many species there are. When looking at human evolution, it is even more awkward. Apart from a few specimens like Lucy, the only fossils are small scraps of skulls, jaws and teeth. It's no wonder that scientists differ in their opinions as to how many species of *Australopithecus* wandered across Africa in the last few million years.

Some fossil experts say there were two species of *Australopithecus*. Others say there were three. Some insist there were four, like we show here. Perhaps it is best, going on present evidence, to think of two main kinds of australopithecine – not necessarily two species. One type would be the *gracile* australo-

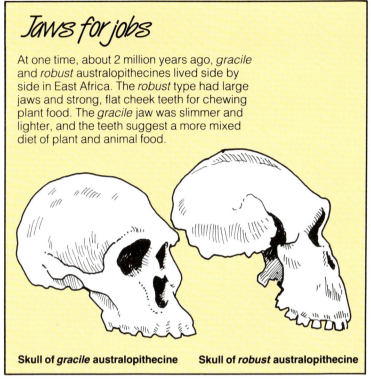

Jaws for jobs

At one time, about 2 million years ago, *gracile* and *robust* australopithecines lived side by side in East Africa. The *robust* type had large jaws and strong, flat cheek teeth for chewing plant food. The *gracile* jaw was slimmer and lighter, and the teeth suggest a more mixed diet of plant and animal food.

Skull of *gracile* australopithecine   **Skull of *robust* australopithecine**

pithecine, lightly built and with a small jaw and teeth. *Afarensis* and *africanus* were in this group.

The other type would be the *robust* australopithecines, including *robustus* and *boisei*. As the name suggests they were larger, of heavier build and bigger-jawed. Both types showed a fair amount of variation between individuals, just as humans do today. They also lived alongside each other at some stage. The *robust* type specialized in plant-eating while the *gracile* type had a more general, mixed diet.

What happened to them? It seems that the *robust* australopithecines were too specialized to be our ancestors, and they probably died out. Perhaps their *gracile* relatives gradually won the battles for food or territories as they continued to evolve, as we can see in the next chapter.

Rooting for food
Nearly two million years ago the robust australopithecines wandered across Africa, looking for food such as roots and fruits.

THE FIRST HANDYMAN

Fossils show that about 1.8 million years ago, in East Africa, there lived a very human-like ape who could make and use tools. This is a human ability. Various animals, including chimps and some birds, use tools such as pebbles and twigs to help them obtain food. But only humans regularly take objects from their surroundings and change them, to make tools designed for a particular job.

The tool-maker from nearly two million years ago has been named *Homo habilis*. Some scientists believe he evolved from one species of *Australopithecus* (page 14). The tool-maker is thought to be related closely enough to us to be in the same genus, *Homo*, as modern man (*Homo sapiens*). The scientific name *Homo habilis* means 'Handy Man'.

'Handy Man' made fairly crude stone tools by hitting one flint against another, in such a way that flakes broke off, leaving a sharp edge for cutting or scraping. Tools like this are very sharp and effective.

At some places where 'Handy Man' tools are found, there are also remains of animal bones. Some bones have marks which were made by cutting – presumably the remains of food which was cut up by using the stone knives.

To go with his tool-making ability, 'Handy Man' seems to have had a larger brain than *Australopithecus*. But he was still only about 1.4 metres tall, like a 12 year-old child today.

Getting ahead!

One of the most famous habiline fossils is this skull, known by its field code number '1470'. When it was discovered it helped to push back the beginnings of true humans by several hundred thousand years, to around 2 million years ago.

The first humans?

Following the discovery of the still ape-like australopithecines in Africa, and the much more human *Homo erectus* in Europe, East Asia and other places (page 23), there was still a gap or 'missing link' in the evolution of humans. The exciting finds of *Homo habilis* filled the gap.

The first specimens of 'Handy Man' (or the habilines, as fossil experts call them) were found in the early 1960s in Olduvai Gorge in Tanzania. More remains were discovered at Koobi Fora, in Kenya, and at Omo in Ethiopia. These fossils were mainly teeth, bits of skull and jaws, found in rocks from 2 to 1.5 million years old. They were somewhat similar to the australopithecine remains that were being found nearby. But it soon became clear that the habilines had bigger brains – 650 mls to 750 mls in volume.

One of the leading anthropologists (experts on human evolution and culture) is Richard Leakey, son of Louis and Mary (see right). He has discovered many remains of *Homo habilis* at Koobi Fora, as well as australopithecine fossils.

As usual, the picture is not as clear as we might hope. Some habiline fossils have big brains but not very human-looking jaws and teeth. Others have human-like jaws and teeth but small

brains. As with *Australopithecus* it may be that there was more than one species of habiline. At the moment, we can't really say for sure.

What we can say is that just less than 2 million years ago in Africa, there were human-like apes with brains bigger than the australopithecines. They almost certainly made and used tools, as you can read on the next page. Gradually the gracile australopithecines faded out. After them, the more specialized, plant-eating, robust australopithecines also died out. *Homo habilis* may have helped to edge them to extinction. The scene was set for the humans to take over.

A fossil goldmine!

Near the wildlife-filled bowl of Ngorongoro Crater, in East Africa, is Olduvai Gorge. This steep valley is 40 kilometres long and in places 100 metres deep. About 2 million years ago the bottom of the gorge was the shore and bed of a lake. Since then it has been covered with layer upon layer of sedimentary rock, trapping and fossilizing whatever happened to be there. Then tremendous earth movements in the area (which is known as the Rift Valley) tore the ground apart to expose these ancient rocks.

Olduvai Gorge (right) is world famous for the discoveries of various hominid fossils, mainly by the palaeontologists Louis and Mary Leakey. Remains of many thousands of other animals, some new to science, have also been uncovered. 'Nutcracker Man' (page 14) was found here in 1959, and in 1960 the first specimen of *Homo habilis* was discovered.

■ = Places in East Africa where fossils of *Homo habilis* have been found.

Olduvai gorge

The Leakeys at work
The Leakey family has been among the foremost fossil experts and discoverers for many years. Mary (far left) examines a reconstructed skull; Louis (left) delicately picks at an embedded fossil; while their son Richard (below) studies a valuable site.

It's easy – with the right tools

The oldest tools in the world are the simple sharp-edged pebbles found at places like Olduvai Gorge. Some pebbles look like knives, possibly used for cutting through tough animal skin to get at the meat beneath. Others are more like scrapers, perhaps for scraping meat off animal bones. These tools were probably used like the Boy Scout's knife of today – for doing whatever is needed at the time.

Prehistoric tools are given certain names depending on how complicated and skilful their makers were. These earliest tools are known as 'Oldowan' (from Olduvai Gorge).

At one time it was thought that *Australopithecus* made these Oldowan tools. Now we believe that *Homo habilis* (Handy Man) made them. It is doubtful whether the small-brained australopithecines were clever enough to select a suitable stone, plan how to shape it, and then carefully chip away flakes to create something that would come in useful for a specific job in the future.

Memory, abstract thought and hand-and-eye coordination are all needed to make tools.

It is unlikely that we will ever catch Handy Man 'red-handed' – that is, find a fossil of *Homo habilis* with a stone tool actually in his hand. So we can never be sure the habilines really did make the tools. But the tools are found in rocks of a similar age to the habiline remains (up to 2 million years old) and in similar places. The conclusion that the experts have come to, is that the habilines were the first tool-makers.

Oldowan tools have also been found in Ethiopia in rocks that may be up to 2.5 million years old. This is half a million years before the first fossils of *Homo habilis* yet discovered. Did some of the australopithecines make tools then? It's more likely that the habilines were alive at this time, and we have yet to find their remains.

Stones *and* bones?
Scientists are fairly certain that the habilines used chipped pebbles as tools. Whether they used broken bones as clubs or gougers is more debateable.

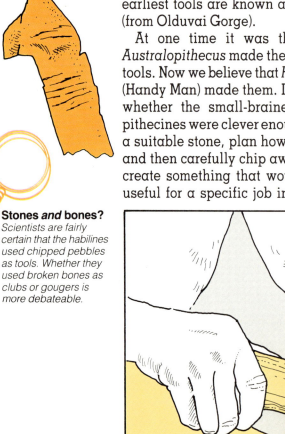

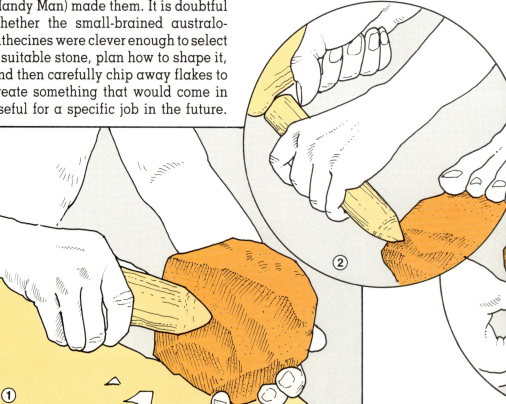

Are big brains best?

Soft parts of animals, such as the brain, quickly rot away and are not preserved. So how do we know the size of a creature's brain from fossils? The answer is that although the brain itself is not there, the space into which it fitted – the inside of the skull – may be. If a fossil skull is fairly complete it is possible to measure the inside volume of the *cranium* (brainbox). By making a small allowance for the fluid and membrane, we can calculate the volume of the brain itself.

But does a bigger brain mean higher intelligence? In living humans this is not necessarily so. Neither is it the case in other animals – or the big whales, with the biggest brains of all, would be far cleverer than us.

Even so, in human evolution the size of the brain and, more importantly, the size of the brain in proportion to the rest of the body, seems to be connected with intelligence.

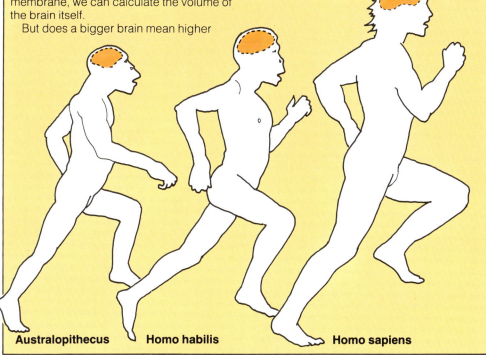

Australopithecus   **Homo habilis**   **Homo sapiens**

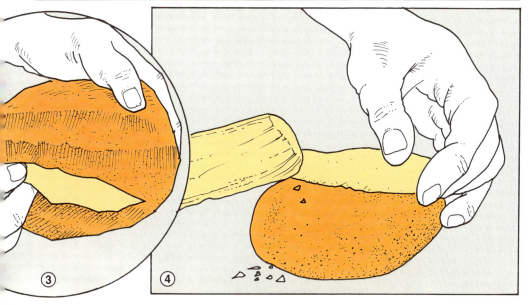

Working in stone
1 *Using a piece of bone or antler as a hammer allows finer shaping of a flint, removing only small pieces.*
2 *Hitting a bone chisel with a hammer gives very accurate splitting of the flint.*
3 *A razor-thin blade of flint is detached by a hammer blow.*
4 *One edge of the blade can be blunted by small taps with a bone hammer, so that it can be held safely in the hand.*

21

OUT OF AFRICA

The early hominids, *Australopithecus* and *Homo habilis*, lived in Africa. The first people we know of who moved out of this continent belong to a group named *Homo erectus* – meaning 'Upright Man'. These people were similar to ourselves in body size. But the main differences were in their skulls and teeth. These have been found to be not quite like those of modern humans, and their brains were only about two-thirds the size of ours.

The oldest *Homo erectus* fossils are from about 1.5 million years ago and were found in Africa, so these people probably evolved there. But by one million years ago they had spread to southern Asia, and later remains have been found in northern China and Europe.

One of the most famous fossils of *Homo erectus* is 'Peking Man' (page 27), found in a prehistoric cave near Peking in China. People like him not only made good stone tools, including beautifully-shaped hand-axes, but they also used fire. The cave near Peking contains the remains of charcoal, burnt bones, and layers of ash. This means that the *erectus* people could use and control fire – probably for cooking, and to help them keep warm in what was a fairly cool climate.

The cave remains tell us that the Peking people had stayed in one place for a time. These upright, tool-making, fire-using humans had begun to have 'homes'.

The first campfires

Northern China in winter can be a cold place. To the 'naked ape' *Homo erectus*, with his early glimmerings of human intelligence and resourcefulness, anything that made life a little easier would be worth investigating. A forest fire started by the lightning bolt of an autumn thunderstorm ... that felt warm ... what if the fire was fed with sticks and kept going in one place? Then the long winter nights might not be so cold.

A far-fetched story, perhaps. But the evidence that Peking Man used fire is strong. We don't know whether he could actually make fire whenever he wanted to, or whether he had just learned to keep a fire going after it had been started by some natural means. Yet the evidence of various finds at caves in Choukoutien and elsewhere gives strong clues to the use of fire. Ash, charcoal and burnt bones have been discovered – presumably the remains of a 'camp fire' and the meal cooked there.

Scorched stones have also been found at the 'camp sites'. Did these people make 'ovens' out of hot stones? Perhaps they dropped hot stones into water, to heat it for cooking. If so, they must have had some kind of water vessel – perhaps even a hole in the ground or a hollow in a rock.

And associated with many *erectus* finds are his characteristic tools. These are Acheulean hand-axes, which are named after a place in France where many have been found. The axes are usually chipped to a pointed pear shape. They first appear in the fossil record about 1.5 million years ago and continue in much the same form for a million years. Hand axes have been collected from many parts of the world, including some parts of Europe where fossils of *Homo erectus* himself have yet to be detected.

Acheulean tools
The well-shaped tools of the erectus people were a great improvement on the roughly-hewn pebbles of the habilines.

 = Places where fossils or signs of *Homo erectus* have been found.

On present evidence, 'Upright Man' seems to have evolved in Africa. Then groups began to spread across the world. They arrived in Europe perhaps 800,000 years ago. These people were intelligent and adaptable enough to survive away from the warmth and plentiful food of the tropics. According to some scientists, *Homo erectus* had virtually died out about 300,000 years ago. Yet in one sense he still lives – since he evolved into us.

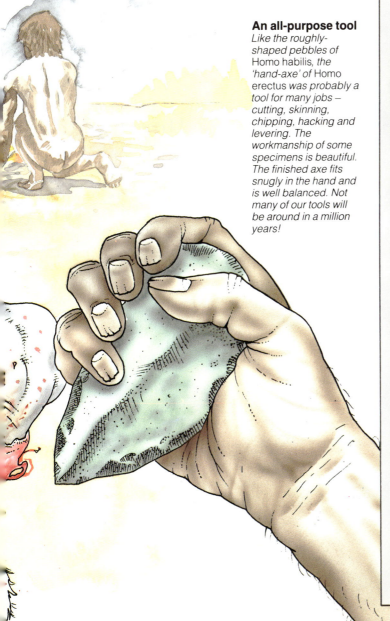

An all-purpose tool
Like the roughly-shaped pebbles of Homo habilis, *the 'hand-axe' of* Homo erectus *was probably a tool for many jobs – cutting, skinning, chipping, hacking and levering. The workmanship of some specimens is beautiful. The finished axe fits snugly in the hand and is well balanced. Not many of our tools will be around in a million years!*

Walking tall

The oldest and most complete fossils of *Homo erectus* were found at Lake Turkana in Kenya, in 1984. Looking particularly at the teeth and the development of the hip bone, the remains are probably of a 12 year-old boy. He was 1.6 metres high – as tall as a 12-year-old boy today.

In fact, apart from the bones being a bit thicker and rougher, they are very similar to ours. The only big difference is in the skull. The forehead is low and there are thick ridges at the eyebrows. This youngster's brain volume was between 900 and 1,000 mls – much bigger than *Homo habilis*, but smaller than modern man's. The body was almost that of modern man, but the brain still had some evolving to do.

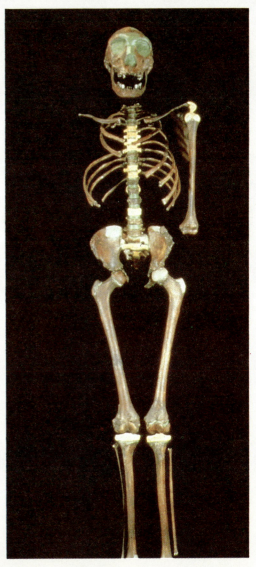

How many 'ape-men'?

Where did we come from? This question has always had a peculiar fascination for humans. Yet delving into the evolutionary clues has not produced a neat, cut-and-dried answer. Fossils of our ancestors are fragmentary, few and far between. Ideas and theories about how we evolved have changed many times in the past, and there is no reason to think we have the right answers now.

Science first started taking evolution seriously when the famous naturalist Charles Darwin wrote about his ideas in his book *On the Origin of Species*. At that time, in 1859, only one type of fossil man had been found – Neanderthal Man (page 34). Virtually all we know today about the various extinct hominids has been discovered in the past hundred years, and much of it only in the past thirty years.

In the early days of fossil-hunting for our ancestors, there was hardly any 'framework of knowledge' into which discoveries could be fitted. There were no similar finds that could be compared, so scientists were free to make their own interpretations. Also, some of the collectors were keen to make a name for themselves and be the discoverer of the fabled 'missing link'. As a result,

Piltdown's discoverer
Charles Dawson was a lawyer who searched for fossils in his spare time. He found the first scraps of fossils on Piltdown Common in 1908.

The hoax of Piltdown Man

The infamous 'fossils' of Piltdown Man were discovered in 1912 in a gravel pit in Sussex, England, by Charles Dawson – an amateur geologist. Over a period of time several fossil pieces were dug up from the gravel. They were brown with age and when put together they formed almost a complete human-like skull and ape-like lower jaw. Many scientists were waiting for such a find – a primitive man from hundreds of thousands of years ago with a large brain but ape-like jaws and teeth. So they hailed the discovery as the true 'missing link', and ignored others who wondered if the skull and jaw really belonged together.

In the 1940s the technique of fluorine dating was developed. Fossils absorb the chemical fluorine from the soil, and the longer they are new species and groups were named on the slenderest evidence.

Hunting for the past has also been affected by the world of the present – several valuable fossil collections were lost in the Second World War, and 'digs' have had to be stopped due to outbreaks of fighting.

New finds are being made all the time. Gradually, though, the picture is becoming simpler. As more remains are found and studied, the experts come to recognize similarities between specimens and we can see the general pattern of evolution more clearly. On the right is a timetable of some of the more important hominid finds in the past hundred or so years.

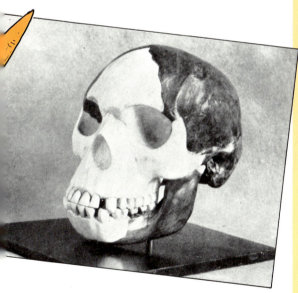

buried the more fluorine they contain. Piltdown Man was tested. The skull and jaw contained hardly any fluorine. Then the technician doing the test noticed that the brown colour was only on the surface of the bones. Underneath they were white and new.

Piltdown Man was exposed as a trick. The remains were actually only abut 500 years old. The skull was of a man, and the jaw was from an orang-utan, with the teeth filed down to make them look human. Both had been stained brown to make them look old and 'planted' in the gravel pit.

To this day no one knows who played this trick, which fooled the world's human evolution 'experts' for over thirty years.

Hominid names – then and now

Year	Find	Scientific name then	Scientific name now
1856	Neanderthal Man	*Homo neanderthalensis* 'Man of the Neander Valley'	*Homo sapiens neanderthalensis*
1891	Java Man	*Pithecanthropus erectus* 'Upright Ape-Man'	*Homo erectus*
1912	Piltdown Man	*Eoanthropus* 'Dawn Man'	(See panel).
1924	Taung child	*Australopithecus africanus* 'South African Ape'	*Australopithecus africanus*
1929	Peking Man	*Sinanthropus pekinensis* 'China Man of Peking'	*Homo erectus*
1938	Kromdraai Man	*Paranthropus robustus* 'Robust Near-Man'	*Australopithecus robustus*
1959	Nutcracker Man	*Zinjanthropus*	*Australopithecus boisei*
1960	Handy Man	*Homo habilis*	*Homo habilis*
1974	Lucy	*Australopithecus afarensis*	*Australopithecus afarensis*

Ancestral ape

Our ancestral past – today!

Before we look at the beginnings of our own species, *Homo sapiens*, let's sum up what we know about our past. The 'evolutionary tree' shown here is one accepted by many scientists – on today's evidence.

Our distant past, possibly involving creatures like *Ramapithecus*, is very sketchy. After this the line of descent runs from *Australopithecus afarensis* through to *Homo sapiens*. As mentioned on page 14, some experts say there weren't four separate species of *Australopithecus* – perhaps two. Also by no means everyone believes that *Australopithecus* evolved into *Homo habilis*. Some say that we should expect to find a 'prehominid' further back in time that was the ancestor of both *Australopithecus* and *Homo habilis*. This would mean that *Australopithecus* wasn't on the line of evolution leading to modern man.

Most scientists believe that *Australo-pithecus robustus* and Neanderthal Man were evolutionary dead-ends. But the idea of *habilis* evolving into *erectus* evolving into *sapiens* has fairly general agreement.

From about 500,000 to 30,000 years ago the picture is confused. Some of the fossils show mixed features of *erectus* and modern man. What was happening? There are two main ideas:

One says that once *Homo erectus* evolved, he spread across the world and then these different groups changed into *Homo sapiens*, perhaps at different speeds. So modern man arose several times in several places.

The second view is that *erectus* evolved into *sapiens* in one place – probably Africa. Then several 'waves' of *sapiens* people migrated to other countries and any *erectus* people already living there died out. Some *sapiens* reached Australia possibly 40,000 years ago. Others went via Eastern Asia into America, perhaps about 30,000 to 20,000 years ago. Still others entered Europe around 30,000 years ago. You can read about these people on the next pages.

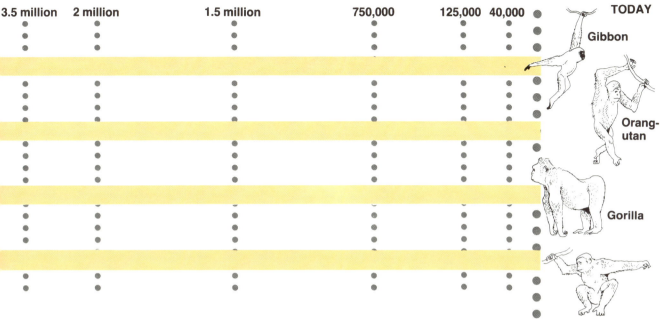

3.5 million	2 million		1.5 million		750,000		125,000	40,000		TODAY

Gibbon

Orang-utan

Gorilla

Chimpanzee

The big split

When trying to sort out our history, it can be helpful to look at the evolution of the other great apes. When did their evolutionary line split away from ours?

Fossil experts used to say that the chimp, gorilla and orang-utan went off on their own evolutionary path about 20 or even 30 million years ago. But the evidence from body chemicals (page 9), as well as a new look at old fossils, puts this split much nearer to today – at 10 to 7 million years ago. This idea of a recent split, say around 10 million years ago, is gradually becoming more widely accepted. If this is true, it means that evolution can work faster than we had thought.

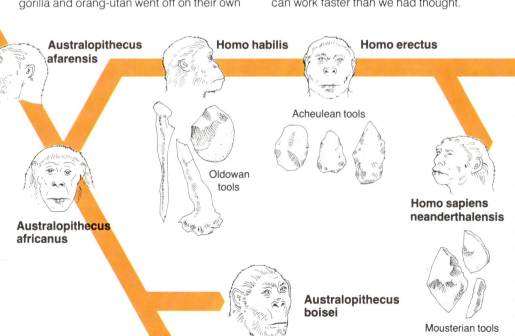

Australopithecus afarensis

Homo habilis

Homo erectus

Oldowan tools

Australopithecus africanus

Acheulean tools

Australopithecus boisei

Australopithecus robustus

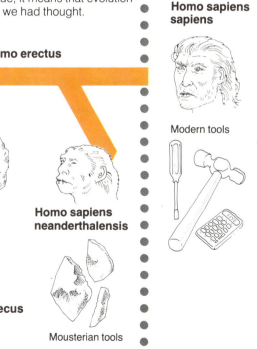

Homo sapiens sapiens

Modern tools

Homo sapiens neanderthalensis

Mousterian tools

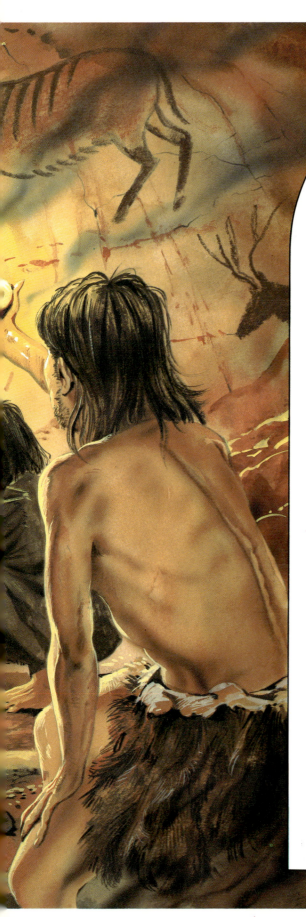

'MODERN' MAN

By about 300,000 years ago *Homo erectus* seems to have disappeared from the fossil record. The first modern humans, of our own species *Homo sapiens*, 'Wise Man', had evolved.

The 'modern' humans looked a bit like the *erectus* people at first. In fact, as more fossils are found it gets more difficult to draw a line between them and us. But gradually the main features of modern humans, such as a flat forehead and small face, had developed. In particular the 'brainbox' part of the skull had grown to house a brain the size of our own, about 1,300 mls.

By 30,000 years ago, remains of humans show that their skeletons were identical to ours today. The people who lived then, during the late Ice Age in Europe, are called Cro-Magnons – after the place in South-West France where their remains were first identified. The remains show us that these people made stone tools of great precision; they crafted useful objects, such as fish-hooks and spear-throwers out of bone and ivory; they sewed skins for clothes and coverings; and they were skilful hunters.

Cro-Magnon people did something else – something really new. They painted beautiful pictures on cave walls. They engraved delicate patterns on ivory and bone, and carved wonderful shapes from wood. They were the first artists.

The Cro-Magnon people

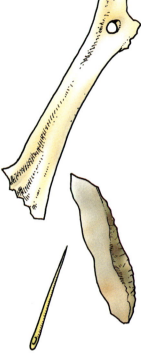

The first Cro-Magnon remains were uncovered in 1868, as workmen dug a railway cutting in the Dordogne region of France. Other remains were found in nearby places and also in Spain. As more discoveries were made around the world, many more finds of similar age came to light. They were between 35,000 and 10,000 years old. Our own sub-species of modern man, *Homo sapiens sapiens*, was truly on the map.

These early modern men seem to have lived in groups perhaps 50 or more strong. With their remains are those of deer, horses and bison – no doubt the results of hunting. While Cro-Magnons lived in Europe the great Ice Age came and went, and there is evidence they hunted the huge woolly mammoths that also lived on the Earth then.

Cro-Magnons left examples of their artistry on cave walls in Southern France and Spain. 'Stone-age' art is also found around the Sahara in North Africa. A great deal of effort went into these paintings. The colours were made by crushing rocks to get pigments. The yellows and reds came from iron oxides and black from manganese oxides. The coloured powders were mixed with animal fats to make paint. Designing the pictures and drawing them in the darkness of a cave must have taken a lot of trouble.

Do it yourself
This early 'tool kit' would allow Cro-Magnon man to carry out a range of jobs around the home. The 'baton' (bone with hole) at the top may not have been a tool, but a symbol of authority.

So why did the Cro-Magnons make their paintings? The animals in them are mostly the ones they hunted, and some appear to have been speared. The pictures probably had some sort of magical or ritual meaning. Drawing a bison with a spear stuck in it could have given you good luck in a coming hunt. The Cro-Magnon people used symbols to express their thoughts. As well as painting, they engraved their hunting weapons with patterns and pictures.

Certain remains appear to be of Cro-Magnon cemeteries. The individuals were placed on their sides with their knees tucked under their chin, and weapons or tools were buried with them. In fact the first skeletons to be discovered had almost certainly been deliberately buried.

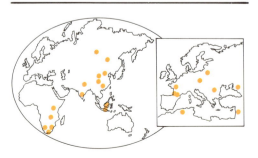

■ = Places where fossils or signs of Cro-Magnon man have been found.

Prehistoric paintings
Cro-Magnon cave art usually shows animals that were hunted for food. The work on the left is from Altamira in Spain; the picture above comes from Lascaux in France.

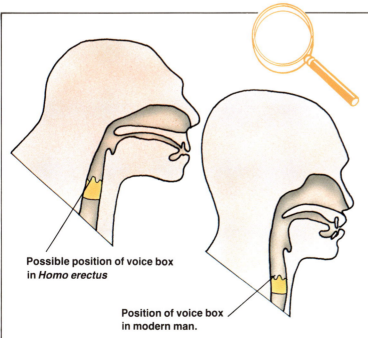

Possible position of voice box in *Homo erectus*

Position of voice box in modern man.

The language of humans

How long have humans been using language? Simple sounds like grunts and screeches were probably used by *Homo habilis* and maybe even *Australopithecus*. But complex languages with hundreds of different words may be fairly recent.

In babies today, the voice box or *larynx* is in a high position up near the skull. Only after a year or so does it sink lower, more into the neck. Then the baby begins to talk. The position of the voice box may be important in speaking clearly. In today's apes the voice box is in a similar high position and never sinks down – and apes can't talk like us.

Fossil evidence shows that in *Homo erectus*, the voice box was also in a high position. So he might only have been able to speak in a clumsy, simple way. Once the voice box had evolved into a more suitable position in the neck, in *Homo sapiens*, better speech was possible.

The cavemen who missed out?

Think of the popular cartoon image of a caveman: short, stooping, stocky and stupid. This image comes from the interpretations of the fossils of Neanderthal Man, but as we shall see it isn't true. The Neanderthals were our very close cousins, belonging to our species *Homo sapiens* but as a different sub-species, *Homo sapiens neanderthalensis*.

Their remains were first discovered in 1856 in the Neander Valley, in Germany. At the time all manner of explanations were put forward – that they were a deformed hermit's bones, or even the remains of someone buried in Noah's flood! But when a nearly complete Neanderthal-type skeleton was uncovered in South-West France in 1908 it caught the world's imagination. The skeleton was reconstructed as a bent, shuffling brute who looked stupid – and who was therefore thought to be stupid.

As more remains came to light the early ideas had to be revised. In 1957 the first skeleton was re-studied. The experts found that this particular Neanderthal Man, who died aged about 40, had suffered from terrible arthritis, and this was what made him bent. The popular picture of Neanderthals had to be changed.

Fossil clues now lead us to believe that Neanderthals were somewhat shorter than we are, but they were also

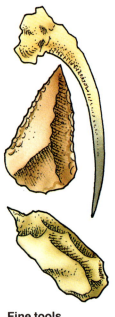

Fine tools

Neanderthal people made fine tools of a type known as Mousterian. There were small and delicate knives, hammer pebbles, scrapers and many other types. With these they hunted woolly rhinoceros, reindeer, hyaena, cave bear, wolf and wild horse.

■ = Places where fossils or signs of *Homo sapiens neanderthalensis* have been found.

much stronger, with powerful muscles and joints, and thick bones. They walked upright, like us. Far from being dim-witted because of the supposed 'small brain', measurements show that the average Neanderthaler had a brain slightly larger than that of modern man's. But he did have a flat, sloping forehead and ridges at the eyebrows that made a rather old-fashioned face.

The skeleton of the arthritic man gave other clues. He was badly crippled and his teeth were so bad he could scarcely have chewed. At the time, during the Ice Age, life would have been tough indeed. How did he make it on his own in such a state? Could it be that Neanderthals looked after each other and cared for their sick? We now know that these people buried their dead. Some graves have wild flowers strewn on them. In others the dead people were painted with reddish earth. Perhaps the Neanderthals believed in life after death.

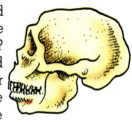

Savage's skull?
The skull of Neanderthal Man, showing the sloping forehead and heavy brow ridges that, at first, made us think of them as stupid and savage.

What happened to the Neanderthals?
The Neanderthal people lived up to 40,000 years ago, during the Ice Age in Europe. Then, quite quickly, they died out. Why? They could have been affected by the climate as the world warmed up again. Or perhaps the waves of modern men migrating across the world killed them off. Then again, it could be that modern people mixed with the Neanderthals and 'absorbed' them by interbreeding.

Fossils of the future

Mankind has come a long way since the first 'ape-men' walked in Africa several million years ago. But we are a very new species on the Earth. Compared to the length of time that dinosaurs ruled the land, or amphibians dominated the swamps, our time so far in the world has passed like the blinking of an eye.

Homo sapiens has spread over virtually the whole Earth. We are changing our surroundings at an ever-increasing rate, and very few areas are now truly 'natural'.

The name we have given ourselves, *Homo sapiens*, means 'Wise Man'. Hopefully it will be more true in the future than it has been in the past, and we will have enough wisdom to mend our ways. If we can avoid nuclear wars, replace some of our natural plant and animal life, and clean up our oceans, we may be able to avoid disaster. If so, what will the fossils of the future look like?

Some evolutionary trends may continue. Physical strength and ability is becoming less important all the time, so our bodies may become weaker and less robust. With less chewing to do our teeth, jaws and jaw muscles may become smaller or fewer.

But our physical evolution is slow. Compared to it, our mental evolution is racing away. In only a few years we have developed computers that can 'out-think' many a human being. Much of our recent past has centred on changes in our thoughts, outlooks and ideas. Perhaps we are entering a new era, when evolution of the body is taken over by evolution of the mind.

INDEX

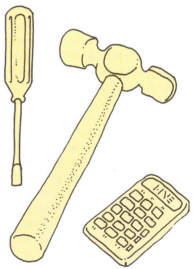